Safe Sledging

Chilly is sledging across the ice. Draw a line to help him get across the ice and back to his igloo without falling down the holes and cracks.

Chilly's Home

D0319426

Dot-to-Dot

Join the dots to find out what Chilly's doing.

Snowman Paper Chain

You will need
A large sheet of white paper
Scissors
Glue, or tape
Felt-tip pens, or crayons

Instructions

1. Fold your large piece of paper, concertina-style, as shown.

2. On the top piece of the folded paper, draw a snowman, as shown.

3. Make sure that the snowman's arms and body go right to the edge of the folded paper.

Spot the Difference

Spot the five differences between the two snowmen.

4. Now, with the help of an adult, carefully cut out your snowman. You need to make sure that you don't cut right around. This is because these are the connecting parts that join the snowmen together to make the chain.

5. Unfold the paper and you should have a chain of snowmen.

6. You can decorate each one with a different scarf. Then, draw on faces and buttons.

Answer: Spot the Difference:

Ice Maze

Chilly is going on an adventure to visit
Santa Claus. Help him get through
the icy maze to find Santa.
Remember to avoid the polar bears.

Chilly
the
Snowman

igloobooks

Snowflake Pairs

Which two snowflakes are the same?

a.

b.

c.

d.

e.

f.

g.

h.

i.

j.

k.

Chilly Fun

Complete Chilly by choosing nose, button, scarf and hat stickers. You could even draw your own snowman and decorate him with extra stickers.

Answer: Snowflake Pairs: b and i

Snowball Fight

Chilly and the children are throwing snowballs.
Who has the most snowballs, Chilly or the children?
Draw some more snowballs onto the picture.

a.

b.

c.

d.

e.

f.

g.

h.

Keep Chilly Cool

Chilly likes to be really cold, otherwise
he will melt.

Draw a ✔ through the cold things and
a **X** through the hot things.

Answer: Snowball Fight: The children have the most snowballs. Keep Chilly Cool: a. X, b. ✓, c. ✓, d. X, e. ✓, f. X, g. ✓, h. X

Draw a Sledge

These children can't join in with the sledge race until their sledge is finished!
Can you shade the children's sledge in for them? You can use whatever pens or pencils you like.

Skate Jumble

Chilly and the children want to go skating, but the skates have got mixed up in the cupboard. Can you help find the five pairs? Draw lines to connect them.

a.
b.
c.
d.
e.
f.
g.
h.
i.
j.
k.
l.
m.
n.
o.
p.
q.
r.
s.

Answers: Skate Jumble: a and h, d and q, f and p, i and m, o and r

Snowman Christmas Scene

1. Slot the background scene (piece a) into slot a on the support.
2. Slot the tree (piece b) into slot b on the support.
3. Slot Chilly the Snowman (piece c) into slot c on the support.
4. Slot the rabbits (piece d) into slot d on the support.

Now you have your own special Christmas scene.

piece d

piece a

Chilly Fun

piece b

piece c

slot d

slot c

slot b

slot a

Coconut Snowballs

These are deliciously simple to make.

You will need
An ice cream scoop
Mini-muffin wrappers
Tray (for freezer)
Foil, or cling film

Ingredients
A tub of vanilla ice cream
A packet of desiccated coconut
A large bar of white chocolate
(optional)

Instructions
1. Scoop out ice cream balls with a small ice cream scoop.
2. Then roll each ball in the desiccated coconut. Place them in mini-muffin wrappers on a tray.
3. Cover with foil (or cling film) and freeze.

Alternatively, you could ask an adult to help you melt some white chocolate. Quickly dip the ice cream ball in the melted chocolate before rolling it in the coconut and freezing.

e.　f.　g.　h.　d.　c.　k.　l.　m.　j.　i.　b.　a.　n.　o.

Keeping Warm
It's important to dress up warmly when it's cold outside. Spot the clothing you wouldn't wear in winter and circle it.

Answers: Keeping Warm: b, c, e, f, g, j, k, m, o

Lovely Lollies

Chilly has bought lollies for the children.
Decorate the lollies using pens and stickers.

Match the Shadow

Which shadow matches Chilly the Snowman?

a.

b.

c.

d.

e.

Answer: Match the Shadow: e

Snowball Fun

a. How many children are throwing snowballs in the picture?
b. How many blue hats can you see?
c. How many icicles are there?
d. How many children have red scarves?
e. How many children have striped mittens?

Now use your stickers to decorate the picture with snowflakes and snowballs.

Answers: Snowball Fun: a=4, b=4, c=8, d=2, e=1

Snowman Gift Tags

You will need
White card
Black card
Felt-tip pens, or crayons
Scissors
A glue stick
Ribbon, or string
A hole punch

Instructions

1. With the help of an adult, cut a hat shape out of black card and a simple snowman shape out of white card. Use the templates to help you.

2. Draw black eyes, buttons and arms on the white snowman shape. Draw an orange carrot nose and add a cosy striped scarf. You can also add some stickers.

3. Glue the black hat onto the snowman's head. Punch a hole through the hat with the hole punch.

4. Thread a piece of ribbon, or string, through the hole, to tie onto the gift.

Then write your message on the back of the snowman.

Snowman Statues

Each of these snowmen have been standing very still, but one has moved. Can you spot the snowman that is not the same?

a.   b.   c.   d.   e.

a.   b.   c.

Follow the Snowflakes

Which line of snowflakes leads Chilly to his hat?

Answer: Snowman Statues: b, Follow the Snowflakes: b

Sledging Fun

Chilly's sledge went down a hill too quickly and he fell into a snowdrift! Can you find him in the picture? Look for his scarf, hat and coal buttons.

Guess Who?

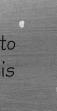

The animals are all pretending to be snowmen, too. Can you guess what animals they are? Here are some animal names to help.

Rabbit

Mouse

Penguin

Polar Bear

Reindeer

a.

b.

Answers: Guess Who? a=Reindeer, b=Polar Bear, c=Penguin, d=Rabbit, e=Mouse

c.

d.

e.

Winter Wonderland

Play this game with your friends.
Each player chooses a different sticker from the book and sticks it onto a coin. These will be your counters and should be placed on the 'START' circle. Then take it in turns to roll the dice and move round the board. The first to the ice palace wins.

START

1

2

3

4

5

6

7
Your sledge is going super fast. Go forward 2 spaces.

8

9

10

11

12
You slip on the ice. Go back 2 spaces.

13

14

15

16

17
Stop to say 'hi' to Chilly. Miss a go.

18

19

20

21

22

23

24

Ice Palace
FINISH